Coloring Book of London,

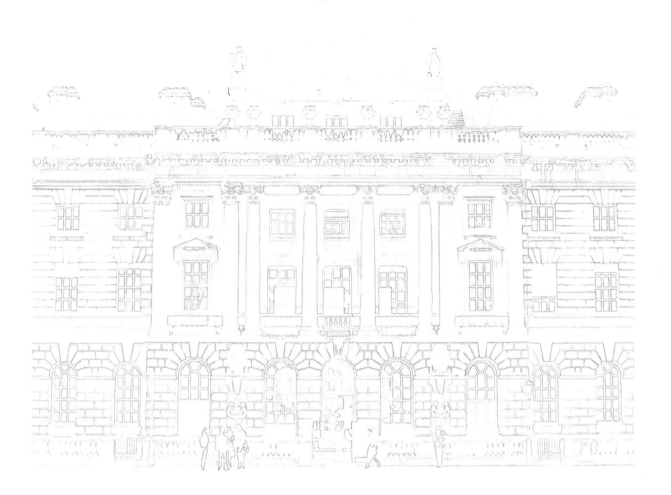

K.S. Bank

Coloring Book of London, England III

Copyright: Published in the United States by K.S. Bank
Published February 2017

ISBN-13: 978-1543207248

ISBN-10: 1543207243

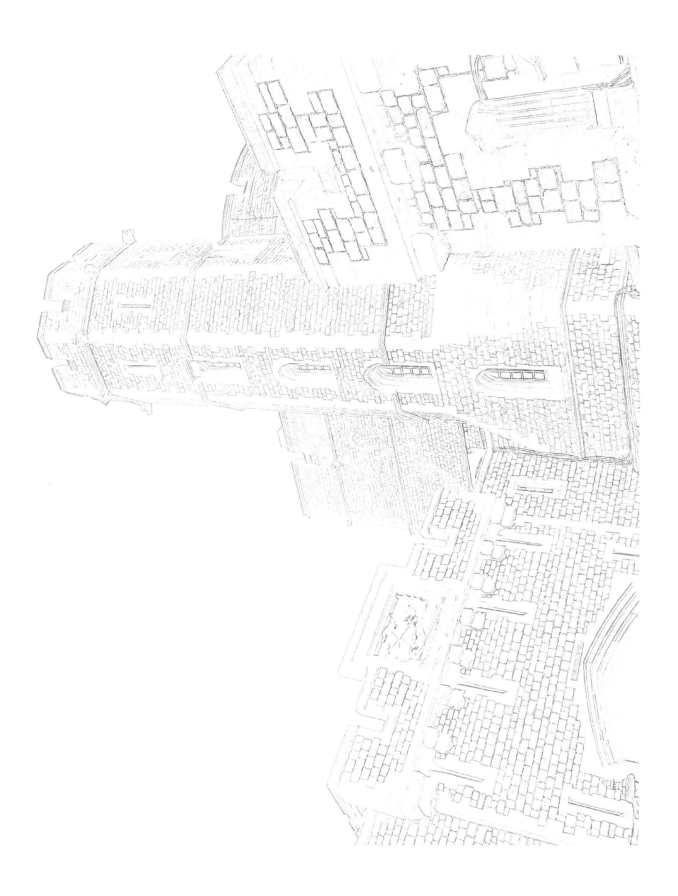

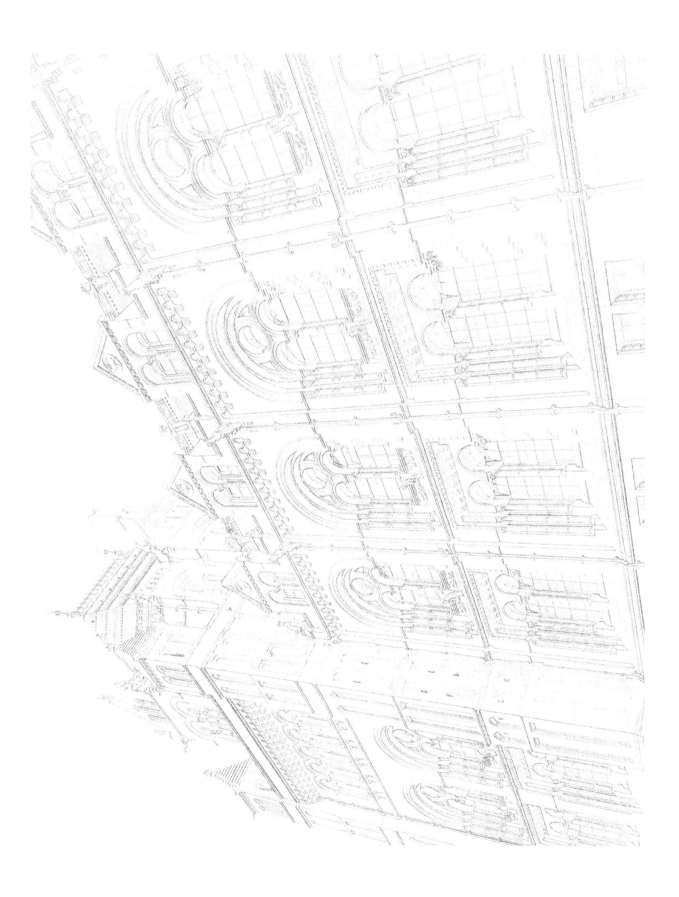

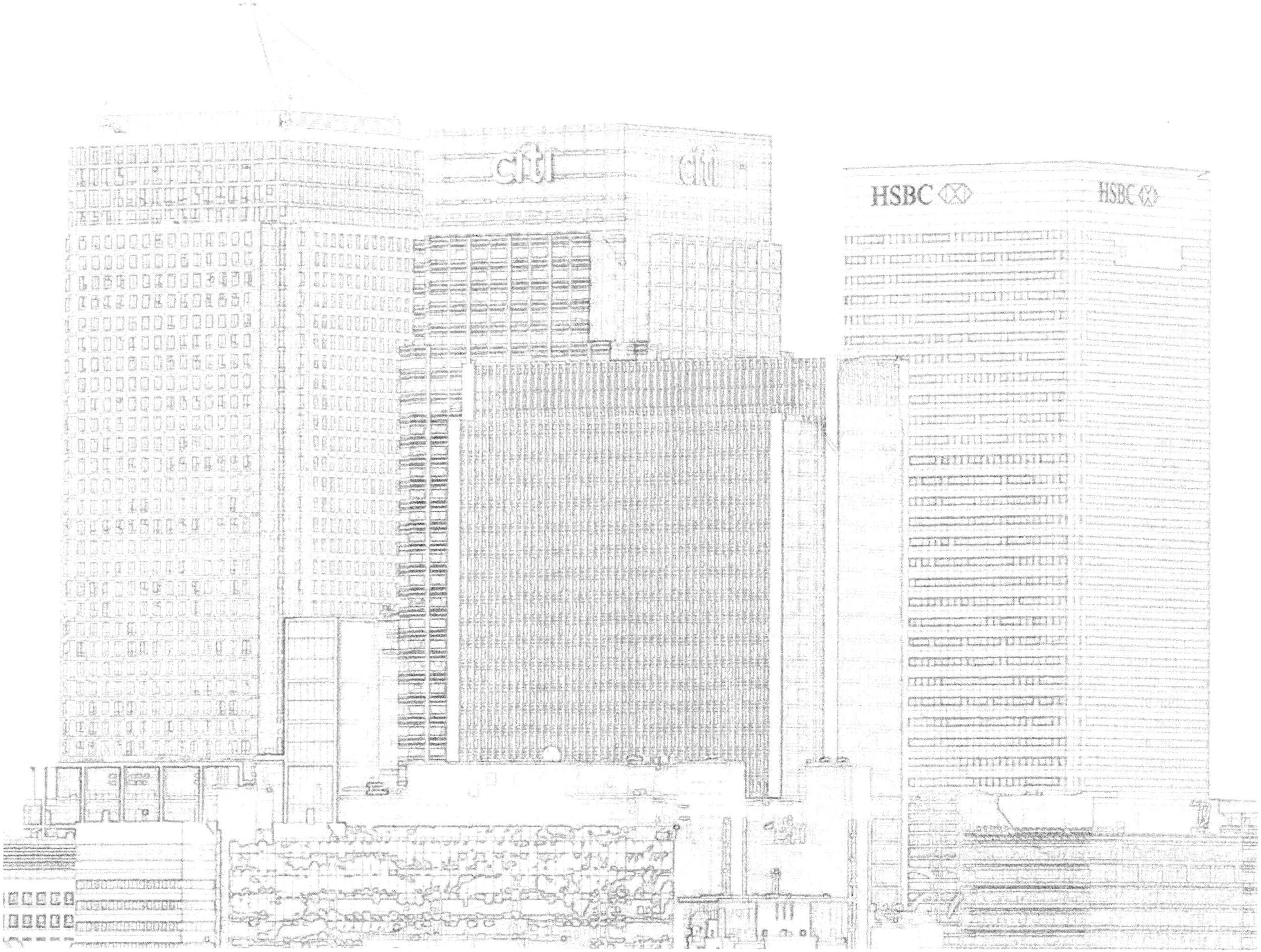
citi
citi
HSBC
HSBC

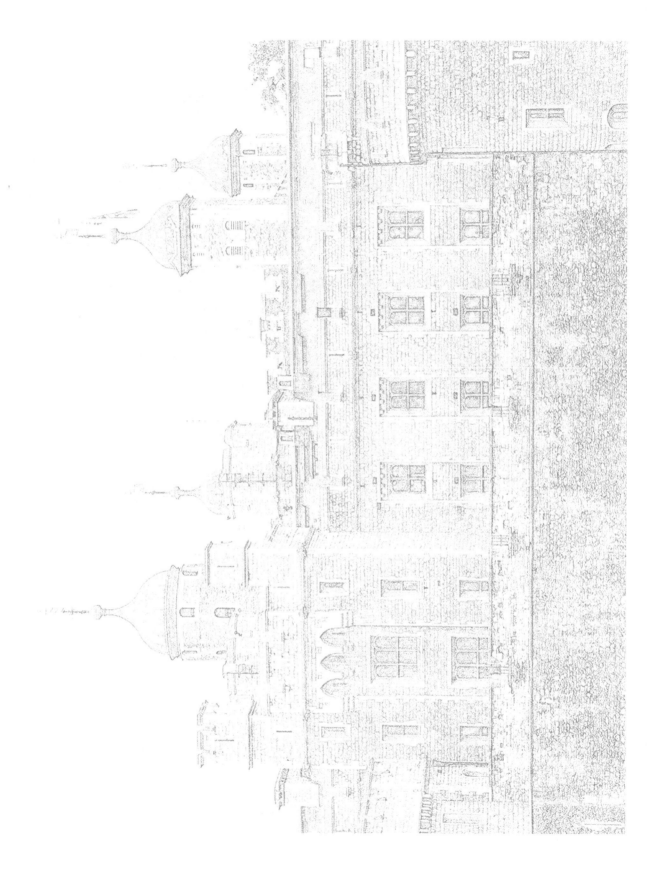

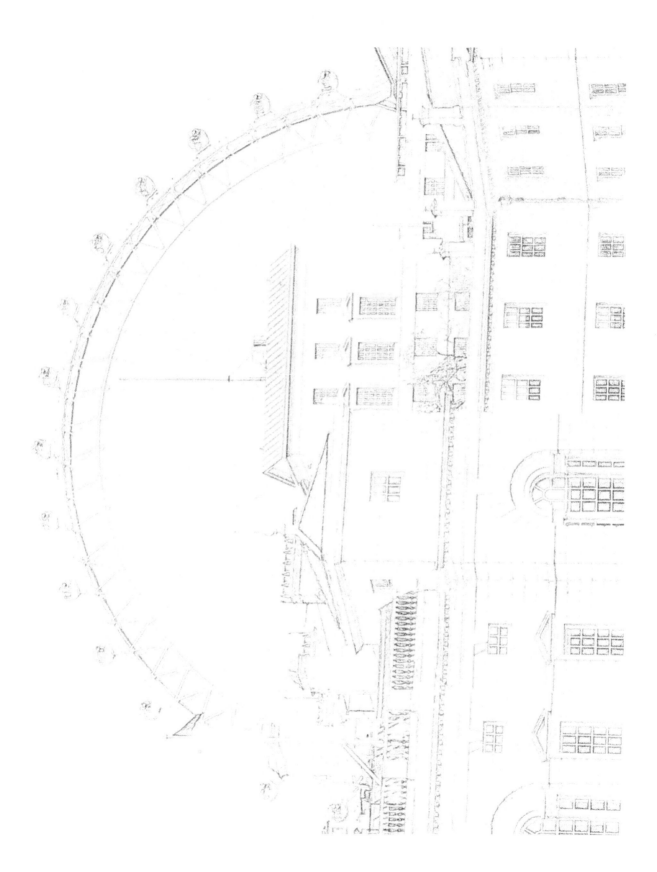

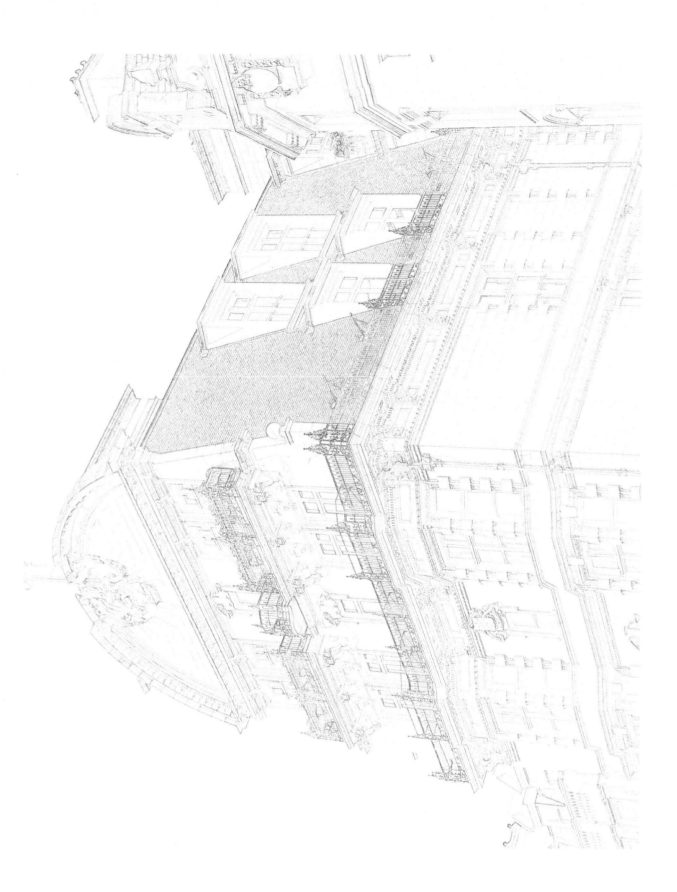

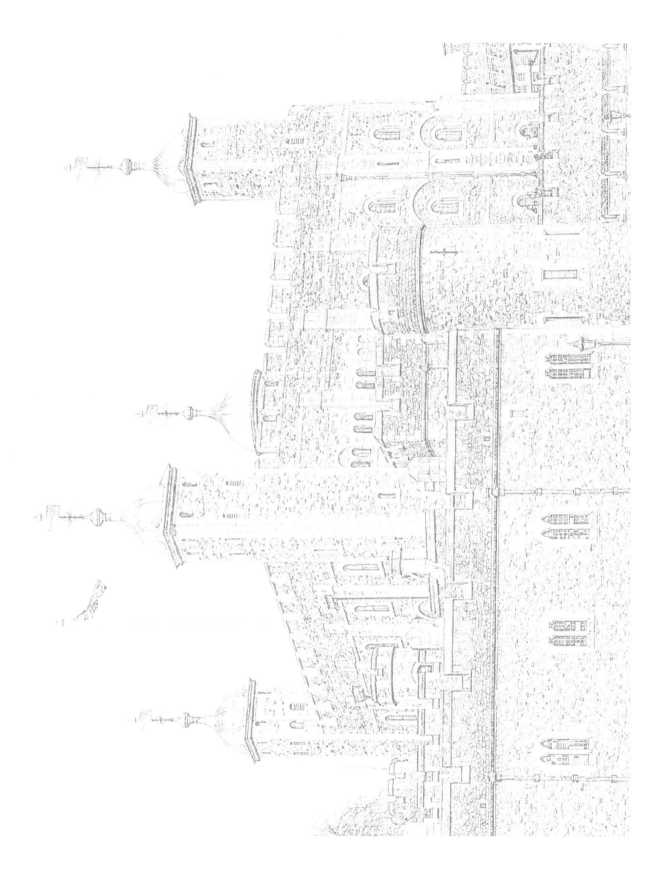

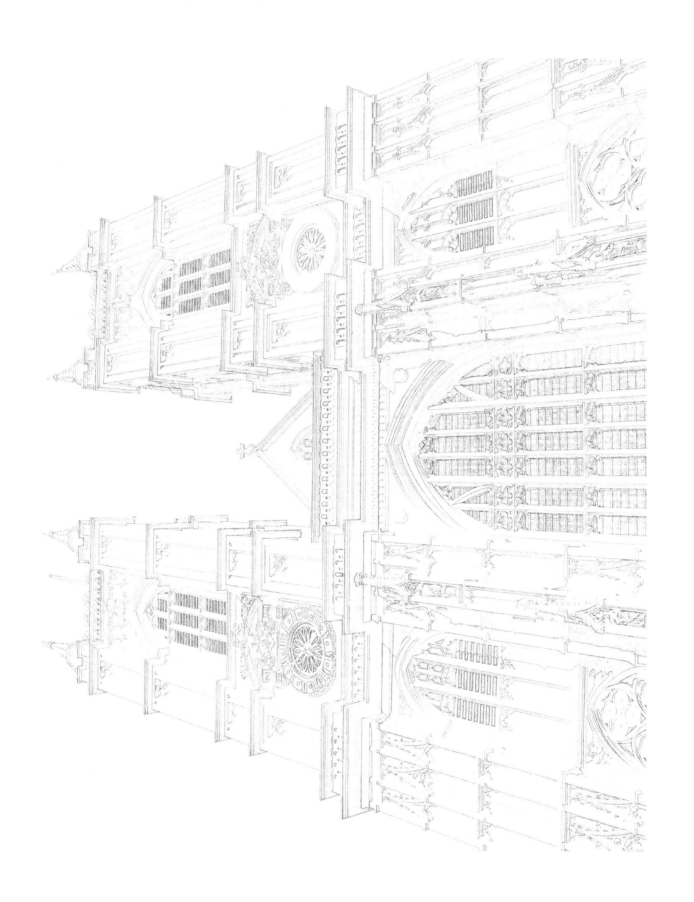

Thank you
K.S. Bank

Made in the USA
Monee, IL
22 September 2022

14481704R00031